PRENTICE HALL LEVELED READING COLLECTION
DISCOVERIES

Working it Out

PEARSON

Prentice
Hall

Boston, Massachusetts
Upper Saddle River, New Jersey

Pearson Prentice Hall™ is a trademark of Pearson Education, Inc.

Pearson® is a registered trademark of Pearson plc.

Prentice Hall® is a registered trademark of Pearson Education, Inc.

ISBN 0-13-361898-6

1 2 3 4 5 6 7 8 9 10   11 10 09 08 07

DISCOVERIES:
Working It Out

How Do We Deal With Conflict?

Table of Contents

The Story of the
ANASAZI

The Anasazi were an ancient race who built an empire a thousand years ago in North America. Their remains tell an amazing story. Years of drought, a period of not enough rain, repeatedly threatened their crops. Famine and enemy raids challenged their communities. Yet, the Anasazi overcame these conflicts and built great cities unlike any seen before in North America. How did they do it?

The Ancient Ones

The name Anasazi means "Ancient Enemy" in the Navajo language. The Pueblo people, who are thought to be the Anasazi's descendents, prefer to use a different name: "The Old Ones," or "The Ancient Ones." The Anasazi were indeed an ancient people and their story is long.

Scientists who study prehistoric peoples believe the ancestors of the Anasazi came from Europe. Around 1200 B.C., they crossed the Bering Strait to Alaska and continued to move south. After many generations, they settled in the North American southwest.

The area where the Anasazi settled is now called Four Corners. It is the place where the borders of southern Utah, southwestern Colorado, northwestern New Mexico, and northern Arizona come together. Four Corners is

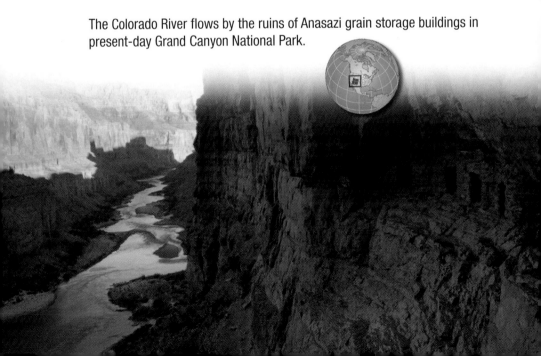

The Colorado River flows by the ruins of Anasazi grain storage buildings in present-day Grand Canyon National Park.

Petroglyphs, or cave paintings, illustrate Anasazi activities.

high desert with deep canyons and towering mesas. Today, it is the site of a Navajo reservation.

The early Anasazi were hunters and gatherers. They did not raise their own food crops. They needed a large area with a mild climate, water, plants, and wild game. That is what they found in Four Corners. The weather was mild, with seasons of snow and rain. It had water, plants, and game. The Anasazi settled in the area and stayed for more than a thousand years.

During this early period, corn from Mexico was introduced to North America. The Anasazi began to plant their own corn. Later they added squash and beans. They became farmers, adding native plants and wild game to their diet. Scientists know this because bone and seed deposits found in archaeological digs **verify** this fact.

Life for the Anasazi was **laborious**. Every bowl, tool, spear, and arrow was made by hand. Everything they wore was made by hand. Everything they ate was prepared by hand. Every seed they planted was farmed by hand. They dug primitive shelters out of the earth, covering them with poles and leaves. In these pit dwellings they lived and died. They dug more pits, known as kivas, where they practiced religious ceremonies. Religion and a belief in many gods were a big part of their lives. They believed that the gods sent the rain.

Then, around 450 A.D., the climate in Four Corners changed. Seasons with some rain alternated with years of little or no rain at all. The streams and rivers dried up. Crops failed. It was a time of great hunger. The Anasazi could have moved on, but now they were farmers. Their own roots went deep into the land. They stayed and hoped that the weather would improve. The weather did improve but not forever.

Periods of drought returned again and again. The Anasazi learned to **adjust** to the changes in climate. They increased the number of crops and grew more food than they needed. They stored the surplus, or extra, food

and used it during times of drought. Still, there was never enough. Skeletons found in ancient burial rites **reveal** that most of the population died of diseases brought on by malnutrition, or not having enough good food to eat.

VOCABULARY

laborious (luh BOHR ee uhs) *adj.* taking much work or effort

adjust (uh JUST) *v.* to gradually get used to a new situation by making small changes to the way you do things

reveal (ree VEEL) *v.* to show something that was hidden

Sunlight shining into a Kiva reveals the wooden beams that help support the structure.

700–1150 A.D.

The Chacoan Great Houses

In the late 700s A.D. came another long and severe drought. During this time, the Anasazi moved into the uplands where rain and snow were usually, but not always, more plentiful. There was a second, darker reason for this move. The drought reduced the food supply for everyone. This caused conflict between those who had little or no food and those who had more. Hungry neighbors began to attack the Anasazi for their food stores. By moving to higher ground and banding together the Anasazi managed to **achieve** greater security.

This Anasazi cliff dwelling contained 114 rooms and housed approximately 100 people.

For the next 200 years, rainfall in the Four Corners was unpredictable. Many of the Anasazi moved again, seeking an area with a more predictable climate.

At that time, the most favorable climate existed in a region now known as Chaco Canyon. Here, the population became densely packed. In time, separate communities organized around a central leadership. Signs of an advanced civilization began to emerge. Artists crafted fine jewelry. Potters developed pottery with beautiful designs. Laborers built roads, which were used for trade. Farmers planted food for everyone rather than a few.

VOCABULARY

achieve (uh CHEEV) v. to be successful in a particular kind of job or activity

Government centers, like nothing ever seen in North America, rose out of the land. Slowly, but steadily, the Anasazi grew into a powerful society known as the Chacoan Anasazi.

Readings of tree rings, which grow fatter during times of good rainfall, **indicate** the climate in Four Corners changed for the better around the year 1000 A.D. Summer rains became more predictable, though not abundant. The Chaco Anasazi already knew how to save and use rainwater sparingly. Now they built dams and canals.

The Chacoan Anasazi were great builders. The government centers, called "Great Houses," consisted of large, arch-shaped, adobe buildings surrounding a central plaza. Some of the buildings rose to four and five stories high. Thousands of huge wooden beams, carried

These Chaco Canyon ruins illustrate the advanced civilization of the Anasazi.

on foot from forests twenty to thirty miles away, supported the heavy structures. The Great Houses included large storage pits for surplus corn, beans, and other crops. The ruling families, artists, and priests lived in the Great Houses. Each Great House included several kivas for religious ceremonies.

The farmers who lived near and beyond these centers looked to the Great Houses for leadership and religious guidance. They depended on the priests to perform the rain rituals. As long as there was rain, the farmers were able to supply the food for the Great Houses and the labor for building projects.

VOCABULARY

indicate (IN di kayt) *v.* to point something out or point to something

Then, in the 1090s, the rains dried up again. During the following years of drought, the Anasazi farmers struggled to produce enough food. Hoping to prevent a famine, the Chacoan leaders built more roads to increase trade with **remote** communities. They built more kivas and the priests performed more rituals. Somehow these efforts **dispelled** the fear of famine. The society stayed together and the weather improved.

Forty years later, a second drought hit the region. Some scientists believe that the farmers finally lost faith in their priests and leaders. Perhaps the farmers believed they would be better off someplace else. They thought that if they moved on, they might find a place with a

This cliff palace is one of many Anasazi dwellings that have been excavated in Mesa Verde National Park in Colarado.

better climate. They hoped to find a place where they could raise enough food for their families. Maybe they realized what their leaders did not, that the great cities had outgrown their resources. Whatever the reason, the farmers began to abandon the city centers. Eventually, there were too few farmers left to supply the food and labor for the Great Houses. By 1150, all the Great Houses were abandoned, too.

VOCABULARY

remote (ree MOHT) *v.* far away from everything else

dispelled (di SPELD) *adj.* driven away; made to disappear

1150–1300
The Cliff Houses

One thing is certain to those who study prehistoric America: the Anasazi were great survivors. Acting on **instinct**, or just common sense, they again sought higher ground. They returned to the uplands where their people had lived three centuries before. It was a good move. Most of their ancestors had left the uplands during the Chacoan expansion. During their absence, the area had renewed its plants and wild game. Now, there was enough to supply food in times of drought.

As before, the uplands, with their high mesas and rocky cliffs, offered security in a dangerous world. Drought and famine were creating tremendous conflict

Cliff dwellings like this one provided shelter and security to the Anasazi.

between those who had a little food and those who had none. Toward the end of the 1200s, the Anasazi had begun to **isolate** their communities within sheltered cliff dwellings. Here they hoped to protect their families from raiding enemies.

Unlike the Chacoan great houses with their open courtyards and open roads, these new communities were closed forts. **Huddled** within overhanging cliffs high above the canyons, the tall adobes clung together in a close embrace. Even today, the cliff dwellings seem **immensely** secure. The cliffs rise beyond arrow shot. It would take only a couple of sentries with dogs posted atop the mesa to spot an approaching enemy.

The Anasazi had learned much about building during the Chacoan period. Many of these cliff palaces were quite large. One, overlooking Guaje Canyon near Los Alamos consists of at least three immense room blocks. Each room had an interior plaza. It had five deep kivas and a number of pit rooms. The pit rooms provided warm places to live during winter. Deep wells held the water supply. In one cliff dwelling, there still remains a well with steps on the inside. The steps circled around and down into the deep earth to a spring below.

VOCABULARY

instinct (IN stinkt) *n.* a natural ability or tendency to behave or react in a particular way, without having to learn it or think about it

isolate (EYE suh layt) *v.* to make a place separate from other places so that people cannot enter it

huddled (HUD uhld) *v.* crowded or nestled close together

immensely (i MENS lee) *adv.* a great deal; very much

The cliff houses were also energy efficient. Nearly all of them faced the sun. The adobe walls absorbed and stored heat from the sun as it crossed the southern sky. During the cold desert night, the walls radiated the stored heat, warming the rooms within.

The farmers used every inch of usable ground surrounding the cliffs. Soil samples **indicate** that they planted crops on top of the cliffs, along the slopes, and in the canyons below. During a raid, the farmers could escape to the fort by climbing the cliffs. Handholds and footholds were carved into the rock face for this purpose.

Today, the most impressive cliff dwelling is found at Mesa Verde. This ancient ruin, hanging high above the canyon floor, is breathtaking in its adobe beauty. Looking up at this golden palace, it seems to be the highest achievement of the Anasazi. This is not so, however. Those days of glory passed away with the Great Houses. The cliff dwellings actually represent the dying breath of a once great culture.

In truth, life on the cliffs was very difficult. Try to imagine the amount of **exertion** it took to build and maintain these high-rise communities. Only then can you appreciate the amount of effort it took to **survive** a dry climate and frequent enemy attacks. Skeleton remains from this period show evidence of overwork, an inconsistent food supply, and terrible violence. It seems the cliff dwellings were not so safe after all. They were completely abandoned within twenty to forty years after they were built.

By the end of the 1300s, the Anasazi had again moved on. They left behind their personal **objects**, such as pottery and tools; their food stores; and even their gods. There is no sure evidence of where they went. They just disappeared—vanished.

VOCABULARY

indicate (IN di kayt) *v.* to point something out or point to something

exertion (eg ZER shuhn) *n.* physical work

survive (ser VYV) *v.* to continue to exist in spite of many difficulties and dangers

objects (AHB jekts) *n.* things that can be seen or touched

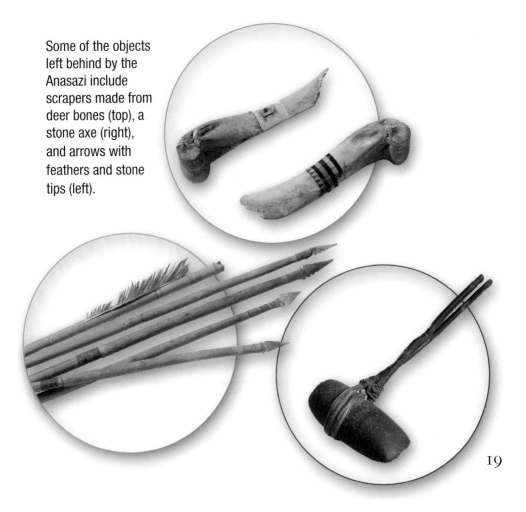

Some of the objects left behind by the Anasazi include scrapers made from deer bones (top), a stone axe (right), and arrows with feathers and stone tips (left).

Where Did the Anasazi Go?

For years a big question surrounded the fate of the Anasazi. The question was not why they left their cliff dwellings. The skeleton remains tell that story. Nor was it how they left. It would be lovely to believe they flew away, as Navajo legend suggests. That is not **credible**, however. Most likely they simply walked away, taking only what they could carry. The one big question that remained was, "Where did they go?"

Handprints like these left in the sandstone verify the existence of the ancient people who once lived there.

Today, after much **research** and scientific speculation, the answer is, "They didn't go far." Most people who study Native American cultures now believe that the Anasazi scattered into small desert communities. They cleverly survived and became the direct ancestors of the Pueblo people. This answer is so **plausible** that few, if any, modern scientists object to it. Still, there may be some truth in the Navajo legend. Perhaps, the Anasazi did fly away, not on wings of feathers, but on wings of hope.

VOCABULARY

credible (KRED uh buhl) *adj.* easy to believe

research (REE serch) *n.* serious study of a subject, that is intended to discover new facts or test new ideas

plausible (PLAW zuh buhl) *adj.* seemingly true; acceptable

Discussion Questions

1. Against what major force did the Anasazi struggle? What other kinds of conflicts did this cause?

2. What action did the Anasazi take to overcome the conflicts that threatened their society? Discuss whether or not their actions were successful.

3. How is the conflict against which the Anasazi struggled similar to a current conflict in the modern world? What are we doing to overcome that conflict?

DISASTER
IN SPACE

Apollo 13 was to have been America's third journey to the moon. When unexpected problems arose during the flight, the astronauts had to face the possibility of dying in space. On the ground, the experts at Mission Control had to analyze problems and figure out solutions in time to save the men on board the spacecraft. How did these people deal with the conflicts they were facing?

Apollo 11 astronaut Edwin "Buzz" Aldrin walks on the surface of the moon.

Just Another Trip to the Moon

On July 20, 1969, the *Apollo 11* spacecraft carried the first humans to the moon. Astronauts made a second successful trip in *Apollo 12* in November of that year. America's **destiny** in space seemed clear. *Apollo 13* was planned as the third moon landing, to take place in the spring of 1970. People began to feel that even **interplanetary** space travel had become routine. One newspaper headline read, "Too Perfect: the Public Is Getting Bored." However, the flight of *Apollo 13* was anything but boring. Something went terribly wrong.

VOCABULARY

destiny (DES tuh nee) *n.* fate; preplanned course of events

interplanetary (in tuhr PLAN uh ter ee) *adj.* between planets

23

Getting Ready to Go

The *Apollo 13* spacecraft had three main sections. The Command Module held couches for the astronauts to sit or lie down. It also contained most of the controls and equipment the crew used. There were five windows in the Command Module. They would give the astronauts a good view on their journey.

The Service Module held much of the fuel for the trip. It powered all the electricity and the engines of the spacecraft. The Service Module was about twice as long as the Command Module.

The third part of the spacecraft was the Lunar Module. It was small and lightweight. It was meant to be used to explore the moon's surface. Three astronauts were chosen to fly *Apollo 13*. James Lovell was the commander. He had flown in space several times before. Ken Mattingly was chosen to pilot the Command Module. The first sign of trouble for the *Apollo 13* flight came when Mattingly, who had been exposed to German measles just before the launch, had to be removed. They replaced him with John Swigert. Fred Haise was the Lunar Module pilot. Neither he nor John Swigert had flown in space before.

The astronauts of *Apollo 13* had many tasks to do on their long trip. They were supposed to **research** and photograph an area of the moon. The information they brought back would help scientists learn more about

James A. Lovell, Jr., commander; John L. Swigert, Jr. , Command Module pilot; and Fred W. Haise, Jr., Lunar Module pilot; pose for their official portrait.

both the moon and Earth. Each astronaut knew his job. They were ready for the launch into space.

VOCABULARY

research (REE serch) *v.* to study a subject in detail, especially in order to discover new facts or test new ideas

Apollo 13 sits on the launchpad moments before liftoff.

Takeoff!

At 2:13 on April 11, 1970, *Apollo 13* blasted into space. The launch took place at the Kennedy Space Center in Florida. Thousands of **spectators** watched in **awe** from the ground. Millions were able to **observe** the launch on television. Everything went as planned.

Two days passed, and the spacecraft neared the moon. On Monday April 13, the astronauts broadcast a television show from space. They gave a tour of the spacecraft. Then, they signed off, saying, "This is the crew of *Apollo 13* wishing everybody there a nice evening."

Down at Mission Control in Houston, everything was fine. The man in charge, Joe Kerwin, reported, "The spacecraft is in real good shape as far as we're concerned. We're bored to tears down here." Then he told the astronauts to flip a switch. This would stir the oxygen in the tanks in the Service Module. The oxygen was used for power, and it also helped the astronauts to breathe.

John Swigert flipped the switch. Then, there was a loud bang. The spacecraft shuddered. It was **apparent** right away that something was wrong. Lights flashed, and alarms went off. Swigert quickly turned back on his radio to establish contact with Mission Control. He said, "Houston, we've had a problem."

VOCABULARY

spectators (SPEK tayt uhrz) *n.* onlookers

awe (AW) *n.* mixed feelings of fear and wonder

observe (uhb ZERV) *v.* to watch someone or something carefully

apparent (uh PER uhnt) *adj.* easily noticed or understood

The people at Mission Control in Houston are able to communicate with the astronauts.

"Houston, We've Had a Problem"

Those **solemn** words struck fear in the hearts of the people at Mission Control. They knew they did not have long to figure out what was wrong. Quickly, they had to **predict** what might happen next. Many of the instruments in the Command Module were not working. Jim Lovell reported that the spacecraft was giving off gas. The craft was having trouble getting fuel.

Within fifteen minutes, it was clear that the astronauts were in deep trouble. An explosion had taken place. Part of the Service Module was damaged. One oxygen tank had blown up, and another was leaking. Mission Control called off the mission. *Apollo 13* would not land on the moon. Serious questions remained: Would the crew be able to get back to Earth? Could they **survive** the trip?

The people at Mission Control thought hard and came up with two ideas. One idea was to have the damaged spacecraft turn around and head straight back to Earth. The engines had been damaged, however. They did not know if there was enough fuel to get the spacecraft back on its own power. The second idea was to have the spacecraft circle the moon. As it went around the moon, it could use the moon's gravity to push it back toward Earth. The spacecraft would be like a pebble in a slingshot, and the moon would shoot it back to Earth.

Mission Control decided to **pursue** the second idea. Nothing like it had ever been done before. The crew and Mission Control had been trained to solve new problems, though. Most difficulties that occurred on a space flight had never happened before. The astronauts and scientists had learned to **react** in completely new ways. They had to be both quick and smart.

VOCABULARY

solemn (SAHL uhm) *adj.* serious; somber

predict (pree DIKT) *v.* to say what is going to happen in the future, based on available information or past experience.

survive (ser VYV) *v.* to continue to exist in spite of many difficulties and dangers

pursue (per SOO) *v.* to continue doing an activity or trying to achieve something over a long period of time

react (ree AKT) *v.* to behave in a particular way because of something that has happened or something that has been said to you

Working to Survive

Inside the Command Module, the crew started to work frantically. They could not spare the time to be frightened. There was too much to do. They knew there would not be enough food or water to get them back to Earth comfortably. They were lucky there was enough oxygen left. However, there was not enough power to run the Command Module. They would have to move into the Lunar Module. The Lunar Module was only meant for two men to use for two days. Now three men would have to use it for four days.

The power in the Command Module began to fail about an hour and a half after the explosion. The crew floated through the tunnel connecting the Command Module and the Lunar Module and closed themselves in. They shut off all the power they did not need. Quickly, the Lunar Module grew cold. The temperature went down to thirty-eight degrees. It was too cold for sleep. The astronauts **huddled** together for warmth. Their feet were freezing, especially Jack Swigert's. He had gotten his feet wet and could not dry them out.

The crew had to use as little water as possible. They knew it would be days before they were back on Earth. They had to conserve a lot of the water on board to cool the spacecraft as it flew. Water to drink was scarce. The astronauts drank only six ounces a day—about as much as a small glassful. They could not cook most of their food without using water, so they could only eat a few things.

VOCABULARY

huddled (HUD uhld) *v.* crowded or nestled close together

This photograph from the movie *Apollo 13* shows the concern of the astronauts for their situation.

Another problem the crew faced was keeping the air clean. When people exhale, they breathe out a gas called carbon dioxide. High levels of carbon dioxide can kill. They needed to think of a way to clean the carbon dioxide out of the air.

The people at Mission Control came up with a solution. They told the astronauts to use duct tape to put together some hoses, cardboard, plastic bags, and cans. They built a device that filtered the carbon dioxide. As Jim Lovell described it, "The contraption wasn't very handsome, but it worked."

John Swigert holds the carbon dioxide scrubber made from parts found in the spacecraft.

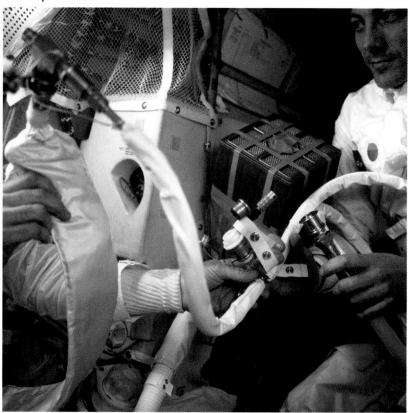

Mrs. Jim Lovell and son, Jeffrey, watch the television coverage of the *Apollo 13* mission.

The World Waits

For the moment, the astronauts had nothing to do but wait. The rest of the world waited, too. The leaders of England, France, Spain, and Japan sent messages to the American government, offering to help. But there was nothing they could do. Soon, everyone would find out if Mission Control's slingshot plan would work.

The crew was tired, cold, and getting weaker. They had to check everything they did over and over again to make sure they had made no mistakes. They tried to **display** strength and courage to the people watching on Earth.

VOCABULARY

display (di SPLAY) *v.* to clearly show a feeling, attitude, or quality by what you do or say

33

Finally, they began their swing around the moon. Now they had to make sure they were headed back at just the right angle. If they were off by just a little, there were two terrible possibilities. If their angle of entry was too shallow, they could skip off the Earth's atmosphere, just like skipping a stone on the surface of a pond. If their angle was too steep, they could burn up as they entered the atmosphere. As they came around the moon, the crew tried to **verify** their course. Because there was so much trash floating around them as a result of the explosion, they could not use the stars to guide them. They had to use the sun. There were long moments of silence. Then, Jim Lovell shouted, "We've got it!" Back on the Earth, Mission Control erupted in a huge cheer.

As the spacecraft headed back toward Earth, the crew fired an engine in the Lunar Module. This would give them the extra push they needed to make it back before their fuel ran out. The engine firing, or burn, worked perfectly, causing the spacecraft to move more quickly toward the Earth.

The final problem the astronauts faced was powering up the Command Module so they could use it to reenter the atmosphere. The Command Module had been **neglected** for days. Mission Control had to invent a way to start it up again. They worked as fast as they could. Ordinarily, this procedure would have taken months to develop, but they figured it out in three days. Powering up the Module was dangerous. The cold had caused water drops to form inside it. When the electricity went back on, there could be an explosion or a fire.

The *Apollo 13* Command Module is displayed after it was recovered.

Finally, Mission Control gave the command to switch on the power. It worked! Then, the crew released the Service Module. As it spun off into space, they finally got a look at the damage the explosion had caused. They took pictures of it. There was a huge hole in the module. They reported to Mission Control, "...There's one whole side of that spacecraft missin'. A whole panel has blown out. Almost from the base to the engine. It's a real mess."

VOCABULARY

verify (VER i fy) *v.* to check whether or not something is true
neglected (ni GLEKT uhd) *adj.* not taken care of

Home at Last

At 7:41 on April 17, the Command Module of *Apollo 13* splashed down. It hit a **remote** area in the Pacific Ocean, just one mile from its target. The three astronauts **emerged** from the Command Module. **Deprived** of food, they had lost a total of thirty-one pounds. Fred Haise had an infection and would be sick for several weeks. Still, they were alive!

John Swigert sits in the rescue basket following the splashdown on April 17.

Fred Haise, Jim Lovell, and John Swigert wave from the deck of the *USS Iwo Jima* after their recovery.

A helicopter picked up the astronauts and brought them back to a waiting ship. The ship took them to Hawaii, where they met their overjoyed families and the President. The next day, the *New York Times* wrote, "The most dramatic space flight in history ended yesterday with the safe return of *Apollo 13*'s crew." The article went on to **emphasize** that the flight owed its success to the "steady nerves, courage, and great skill" of the astronauts and the people at Mission Control.

VOCABULARY

remote (ree MOHT) *adj.* far away from everything else

emerged (ee MERJD) *v.* came out from somewhere

deprived (dee PRYVD) *adj.* not having the things that are necessary

emphasize (EM fuh syz) *v.* to show that an opinion, idea, or quality is especially important

Why did *Apollo 13* fail? A panel of experts was appointed to find out. They discovered that in 1965, the Command Module had undergone some changes. The amount of electricity that went to the heaters in the oxygen tanks had increased. This caused the temperature in the tanks to rise, too. However, the temperature controls that were supposed to switch off the heaters when the tanks got too hot were not changed. The heaters were on for a long period of time during a test just before the launch. Because the temperature controls did not work right, they overheated the wiring near them. The oxygen tanks were like a bomb, ready to go off. When Jack Swigert flipped the switch to stir the oxygen, a spark must have caused the tank to explode.

Jim Lovell reads a newspaper account of the safe recovery.

Apollo 13 reminded everyone that travel into space was anything but routine. However, the fact that the spacecraft had made it back home, with all the astronauts alive, showed that the minds behind the space program were able to wrestle with and solve the complex and dangerous problems that could arise at any moment. As Jim Lovell put it, "Our mission was a failure, but I like to think it was a successful failure."

Discussion Questions

1. Following the explosion aboard *Apollo 13,* Mission Control had to make a decision: Should they call off the mission or not? Debate the argument "for" and "against" calling off the mission.

2. Mission Control also faced the problem of returning the astronauts safely to Earth. Describe the plan Mission Control put into place. Debate the argument "for" and "against" this approach.

3. Do you think you would be able to make decisions like the ones Mission Control had to make? Why or why not?

From the days of slavery, African Americans used music to express their hardships and hopes. Blues music became part of that tradition. Singing the blues was a way of dealing with the daily struggles caused by discrimination and racism. For blues singers and musicians, it could also be a way of coping with personal pain. Playing or singing the blues might not fix a problem, but it creates a powerful way of expressing conflict.

Singin' Away

Celebrating the Blues

You probably did not know that 2003 was the "Year of the Blues." The United States Congress named the year to recognize the 100th anniversary of the blues. In a **solemn** proclamation, Congress called the blues "the most influential" and "the most celebrated form of American roots music."

Early blues musicians could hardly have imagined such an honor. The blues, after all, was a form of music that developed from the oppression of African Americans. You probably know that the phrase *feeling blue* means "to be sad." The whole idea of blues music is that playing, singing, or listening to the blues can help get rid of sad feelings. Music can provide **consolation** for performers and audiences. When you are suffering, it helps to get those feelings out. It also helps to know you are not alone.

VOCABULARY

solemn (SAHL uhm) *adj.* serious; somber

consolation (kahn suh LAY shuhn) *n.* something that comforts a disappointed person

This replica of slave quarters in Baton Rouge, Louisiana, shows the poverty in which many people lived.

The Birth of the Blues

No one knows for sure who created the first blues music. Music experts trace it to several areas of the South in the years following the Civil War. Blues music developed from field songs and spirituals sung by slaves. It was a response to the injustices that free blacks experienced after slavery ended. Freedom did little to help them **attain** better lives.

Many blacks worked the fields of large farms as sharecroppers. They were paid with a share of the crops they grew, but that was usually only enough to survive. They were still poor and still mistreated. Beginning in the 1880s, laws in many parts of the country made discrimination legal. Blacks, especially in the South, were still trapped by **malicious** prejudice.

By the early 1900s, blues music had caught on in places like the Mississippi Delta. It was down-home music with a unique sound.

W.C. Handy: Father of the Blues

The blues is given the "birth year" of 1903 thanks to William Christopher Handy, known as W.C. As the story goes, Handy was waiting on a train platform in Tutwiler, Mississippi, one night in 1903. He heard a poor black man singing. According to Handy, it was "the weirdest music" he ever heard. Blues music typically has two lines that are repeated and then a third line. Here is an example from a blues song called "Bad Luck Blues."

> *Hey people, listen while I spread my news.*
> *Hey people, listen while I spread my news.*
> *I wanna tell you people all about my bad luck blues.*

Even though Handy found the man's song strange, he could **appreciate** the new style and he could connect with many of the emotions behind the blues.

VOCABULARY

attain (uh TAYN) *v.* to succeed in reaching a particular level or in getting something after trying for a long time

malicious (muh LISH uhs) *adj.* spiteful; hateful

appreciate (uh PREE shee ayt) *v.* to understand or enjoy the good qualities or value of someone or something

43

W.C. Handy plays the cornet for an audience.

Handy was born in Alabama in 1873, fewer than ten years after the Civil War. His parents had been slaves. The family lived in a log cabin built by his grandfather. Handy grew up loving music. He could pick out the notes and rhythms of sounds in nature. However, music was also a source of conflict. His father and grandfather did not approve of music. When Handy saved money and bought a guitar, his father made him return it. Imagine how **devastating** it must have been for Handy. He desperately wanted to play music. He had the talent. No wonder he understood the blues when he heard it years later.

Handy followed his father's wishes and became a teacher. However, black teachers were paid poorly. Eventually, Handy began making a living from what he loved — music. He played in bands and minstrel shows, which were like variety shows with music, dancing, and comedy. He traveled widely throughout the country as a musician and then as a band and orchestra leader.

Early blues music was not written down. Handy changed that. His first blues song, known as "Memphis Blues," was published in 1912. Two years later, he wrote "St. Louis Blues," which became his most famous work.

Handy helped to bring the blues into the spotlight. He **coaxed** it from a made-up, **impromptu** kind of music into a recognized form. Handy wrote many orig-inal blues songs during the 1920s and 1930s. He also wrote down popular blues songs. He published books about the blues and black composers.

VOCABULARY

devastating (DEV uh stayt ing) *adj.* destructive; overwhelming
coaxed (KOHKST) *v.* used gentle persuasion
impromptu (im PRAHMP too) *adj.* unscheduled; unplanned

Handy achieved great success. Yet, he still had personal struggles worthy of a blues song. He went totally blind after falling from a subway platform in New York City in 1943. Despite that, Handy's life was easier than life for many African Americans of his time. He was honored for his career and for creating an audience for the blues. Many blues singers had deeper troubles to sing about.

Bessie Smith: Empress of the Blues

Bessie Smith was born in Chattanooga, Tennessee, in 1894. Both her parents died when she was a child. Her oldest sister raised her. Young Bessie was singing on street corners in Chattanooga at the age of nine. By the time she was a teenager, she was singing in variety shows.

Smith had a lot of bad luck in her early life. However, she got one very good break. She appeared in a show with Ma Rainey, a well-known blues singer. Rainey recognized the younger woman's talent and helped her along. Rainey understood how much Smith had to offer. Bessie Smith **displayed** amazing power and passion when she sang. Her voice carried her to great heights before her career burned out.

VOCABULARY

displayed (di SPLAYD) v. clearly showed a feeling, attitude, or quality by what you did or said

46

Bessie Smith, shown here, was the most successful female blues singer of the 1920s.

Smith started as a traveling singer in the South. It was a difficult life. She was not entertaining in fancy clubs. She sang in tents and run-down theaters. Still, no one could **ignore** her talent. She became a top performer in black touring shows. Smith recorded her first blues song, called "Down-Hearted Blues," in 1923. It was a huge success.

Smith became a superstar in her time. She was the "Empress of the Blues" and the best-known black performer in the 1920s. Smith recorded many songs and continued to tour in both the South and the North. Now she was singing for bigger audiences. She even appeared in the movie *The St. Louis Blues*, in 1929.

Smith sang blues songs about all kinds of misery. Her songs had titles like "House Rent Blues," "Sobbin' Hearted Blues," "Careless Love Blues," "Money Blues," and "I Ain't Gonna Play No Second Fiddle." The titles **demonstrate** the nature of blues music. It was about troubles. Even at the height of her success, Smith knew all about troubles. Conflict was a constant in her life. She developed a drinking problem as a young woman. Her first husband died soon after their marriage in 1920. Her second marriage was unhappy and ended in divorce.

Decline of the Blues By the 1930s, blues music was no longer as popular as it had been a decade earlier. Smith's career tumbled. Her **perpetual** drinking made everything worse. She died in a car accident in Clarksdale, Mississippi, in 1937.

When Smith sang songs like "Nobody Knows You When You're Down and Out," she sang like she meant it. Blues music expressed the struggles of African Americans. It also conveyed many individual sorrows.

VOCABULARY

ignore (ig NOHR) *v.* pay no attention to

demonstrate (DEM uhn strayt) *v.* to show or prove something clearly

perpetual (puhr PECH oo uhl) *adj.* constant; unending

Billie Holiday: Lady Sings the Blues

Billie Holiday titled her autobiography *Lady Sings the Blues*. She was one of the best blues and jazz singers. She had plenty of blues to sing about.

Holiday's life was full of chaos and conflict from the start. She was born in 1915 in Philadelphia, Pennsylvania. Her parents were teenagers when she was born and split up when she was young. Many details of Holiday's early life are not clear. She moved with her

Billie Holiday performs onstage.

mother to Baltimore, Maryland. Then, she lived with relatives when her mother went to New York. Holiday claimed she was treated badly by her relatives. She had little schooling and dropped out. She eventually moved to New York to be with her mother. There was nothing **timid** about young Billie. She was tough.

VOCABULARY

timid (TIM id) *adj.* showing shyness

Holiday also had an amazing singing voice, and people soon discovered it. In the early 1930s, she began performing in clubs in Harlem, the celebrated African American neighborhood of New York. By then, the blues had helped create the livelier musical sound of jazz. Holiday quickly became a popular jazz singer. However, she could also do justice to the blues. Her voice had the same kind of emotional power that Bessie Smith's had. Holiday could **emphasize** just the right words and notes to make a song touch the heart.

In the blues tradition, Holiday sang about pain and injustice. Songs such as "God Bless the Child" and "Gloomy Sunday" expressed not only her great talent, but her incredible pain as well.

Like Smith, Holiday's own struggles overwhelmed her singing talent. Her song "Good Morning Heartache" could describe many of her days. She had difficult personal relationships and problems with drugs. She tried to continue her career and had successful concerts in Europe in the 1950s. Unfortunately, she also continued to **rely** on people who took advantage of her and on drugs. She died at the age of forty-four.

Holiday is remembered for a voice that could convey the mood and meaning of a song. She was part of a changing time in the blues scene.

B.B. King: King of the Blues

Many young people who enjoy blues music today can probably thank B.B. King. In 50 years as a blues musician, this legendary artist has helped bring the blues into mainstream music. King's own history has a setting and **plot** similar to the story of blues music. He was born in Mississippi in 1925. His family was poor, and he

VOCABULARY

emphasize (EM fuh syz) v. to show that an opinion, idea, or quality is especially important

rely (ree LY) v. to trust someone or something to do what you need or expect them to do

plot (PLAHT) n. the sequence of events in a story

worked as a sharecropper as a boy. King's mother and grandmother were religious, and church was an important part of his life. He grew up on gospel songs and the early blues music of the Mississippi Delta.

King's musical career began in 1946, when he moved to Memphis, Tennessee. Beale Street in Memphis is called "the home of the blues." King had a cousin there who was a blues guitarist. King learned to play the guitar. He also gained his nickname in Memphis. He was known as the Beale Street Blues Boy — shortened to B.B.

Much of King's pioneering work was on the electric guitar. He was one of the first to **exhibit** a talent known as "bending the strings." It gave his blues guitar music more power and greater emotion. His style went on to influence pop and rock performers from the 1960s until today.

"The Thrill Is Gone" was King's first blues song to hit the top of the pop charts, in 1969. For those who gained a new appreciation for the blues through King's music, the thrill was just beginning. They could safely **anticipate** many more songs. King did not disappoint. In fact, he celebrated his eightieth birthday in 2005 with a new album.

VOCABULARY

exhibit (eg ZIB it) *v.* to show a particular quality, sign, or emotion so that it is easy to notice

anticipate (an TIS uh payt) *v.* to expect an event or situation to happen, and do something to prepare for it

B.B. King performs with his guitar "Lucille" in Bonn, Germany.

A slave family is painted on the door of this slave quarters at the Rural Life Museum in Louisiana.

The Blues Today

Blues began as a musical voice for African Americans to speak about suffering and injustice. As blues music changed in the twentieth century, so did the lives of African Americans. The Civil Rights Movement helped end legal discrimination. Education and interaction among the races have helped lessen prejudice.

Yet, blues music is still about expressing the strong feelings of conflict. Today, a broader audience may know a few B.B. King classics like "Paying the Cost to Be the Boss," "How Blue Can You Get," and "When Your Baby Packs Up and Goes." This vibrant music called the blues will continue to be appreciated as long as people have troubles and heartache to express.

Discussion Questions

1. Blues music is based on the idea that performing or listening to the blues helps release sadness. Does this idea make sense as a way to deal with external or internal conflict? Explain your point of view.

2. Think about the four blues performers spotlighted in the article. What do they have in common? Why do you think audiences are drawn to certain blues artists? Explain.

3. How might music help you deal with conflicts? Explain.

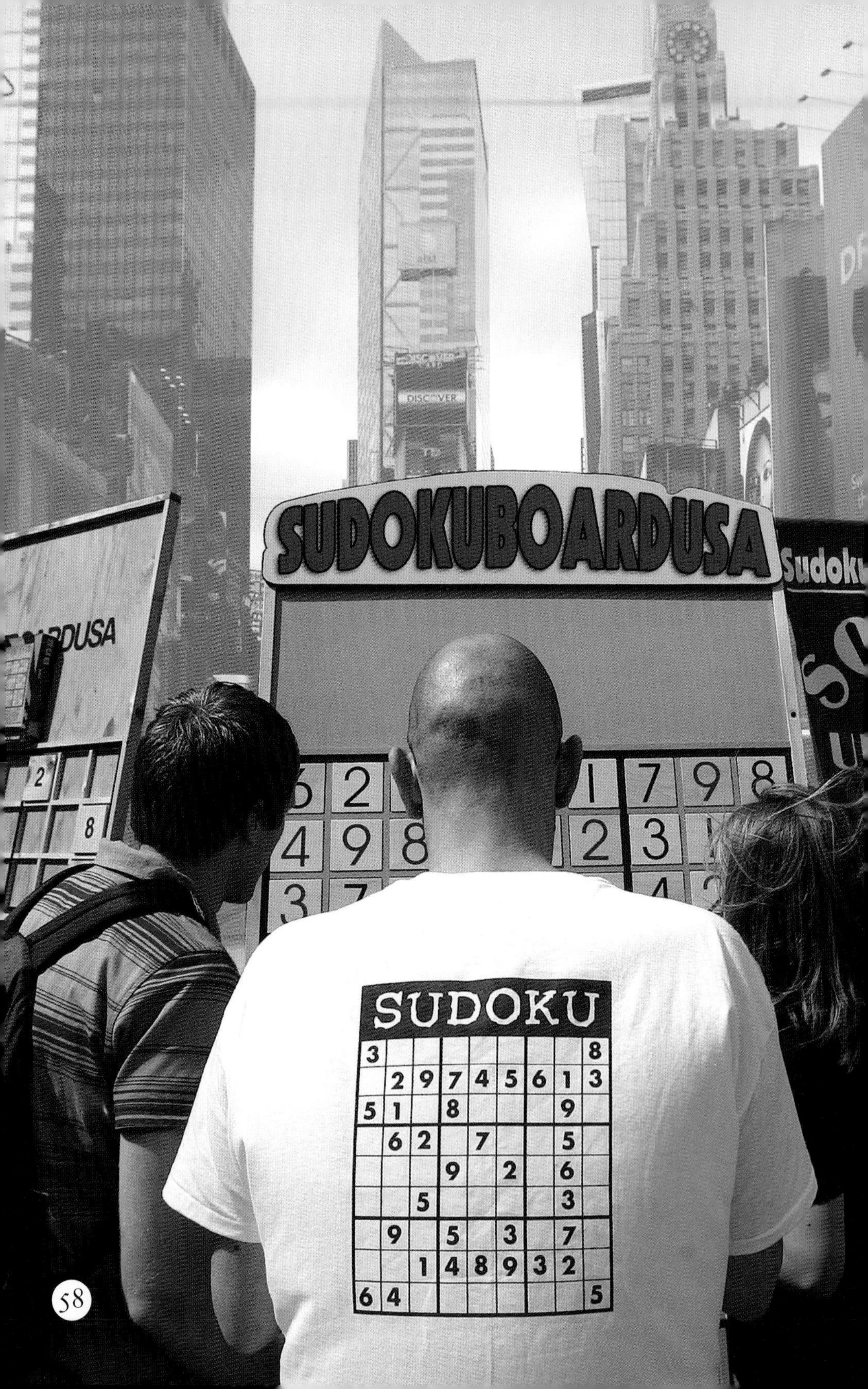
SUDOKUBOARDUSA
Sudoku
DISCOVER
SUDOKU

SOLVING SUDOKU

数独

Why do people do puzzles? Puzzle expert Will Shortz points out that they "give the solver a feeling of being in control. Most of life's challenges don't have black-and-white solutions, and many have no resolution at all." Puzzles, on the other hand, present conflicts that always have one perfect solution. No matter how difficult a puzzle seems, you know that there is an answer. A simple grid of numbers and squares has people around the globe asking the same question:

"Can you solve Sudoku?"

The Sudoku Story

Howard Garns created the first Sudoku [soo DOH koo] puzzle in 1979. However, he called it Number Place. It was a variation of a math game known as Latin Squares. Five years later, the puzzle was picked up and renamed by a Japanese newspaper. "Sudoku" is a short form of a Japanese phrase that means "only single numbers allowed."

In 1997, a retired judge named Wayne Gould saw a Sudoku puzzle. He was so fascinated by the game that he designed a computer program to create the puzzles. Then, he decided to **promote** his favorite game. In 2004, he persuaded *The Times,* a London newspaper, to publish Sudoku games. Soon, other British newspapers began to print their own versions of the popular game. The Sudoku fad was launched.

Pencil Popularity Within a year, Sudoku was called "the fastest growing puzzle in the world." Publishers have sold more than 5.7 million copies of Sudoku books. Many newspapers now publish two puzzles every day: one easy and one challenging. If that does not **impress** you, maybe this fact will. Pencil sales in London increased by 700 percent as a result of the Sudoku craze!

In July 2005, the Sky One television network presented Sudoku Live. Nine teams of nine players competed as they **simultaneously** solved puzzle after puzzle. One ad for the show

Wei Hwa Huang takes part in the first World Sudoku Championship in Lucca, Italy.

was a giant Sudoku puzzle carved into a hill in England. Unfortunately, the puzzle design was flawed. There were 1,905 correct solutions.

First World Championship The first World Sudoku Championship took place in March 2006 in Lucca, Italy. The contest attracted 85 expert solvers from 22 countries. They were between ages 15 and 61. Players faced both traditional Sudoku puzzles and some tricky new variations. The winner was Jana Tylova, an accountant from the Czech Republic. She received her trophy from Wayne Gould, the man who helped to **establish** Sudoku as a true worldwide craze.

Vocabulary

promote (pruh MOHT) *v.* to help something develop and be successful

impress (im PRES) *v.* to affect someone, especially by making them feel admiration and respect for you

simultaneously (sy muhl TAY nee uhs lee) *adv.* at the same time

establish (uh STAB lish) *v.* to make sure of; to determine

The Rule of Sudoku

What is Sudoku? A Sudoku puzzle has a grid with 9 rows and 9 columns. The grid is also divided into 9 3x3 blocks. This diagram **illustrates** the Sudoku board. It also names the rows, columns, and blocks. Learning these names will help you understand Sudoku solution strategies.

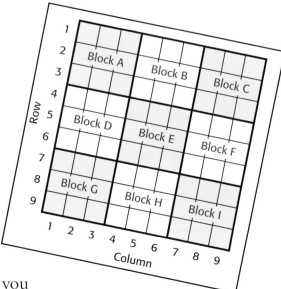

Notice that the blocks are named with letters instead of numbers. This can make it less confusing to talk about positions on the grid.

Why is Sudoku so popular? One reason is that it is very easy to understand. In fact, there is really just one important Sudoku rule. Here it is:

Each digit from 1 to 9 appears once—and only once—in each row, column, and block.

Look at this Sudoku solution. You can test how this rule works. Pick a row and find each digit from 1 to 9. Then, pick a column and find each digit.

Finally, choose a block and **verify** that it contains each digit only once.

That is the simple rule behind every Sudoku puzzle. As you will see, one simple rule can lead to puzzles that are surprisingly **intricate**.

Of course, a Sudoku puzzle does not come with all of the numbers filled in. A lot of the squares are empty. Only a few of the numbers are shown. These numbers are called the "givens." The givens are all you need to find a complete solution.

Sudoku is a puzzle of logic, not guessing. Your goal is to fill in all of the squares. You can **accomplish** this task by using logic. Follow an organized plan and you can uncover the missing numbers. Try find the digits that complete this puzzle.

One basic Sudoku hint is to use a pencil. The eraser comes in very handy when you make a mistake.

VOCABULARY

illustrates (IL uh strayts) *v.* to make the meaning of something clearer by giving examples

verify (VER uh fy) *v.* to check whether or not something is true

intricate (IN tri kit) *adj.* complex; detailed

accomplish (uh KAHM plish) *v.* to succeed in doing something, especially after trying very hard

Scanning to Solve

To solve Sudoku puzzles, you will need to scan the grid for information. There is no "best" way to solve Sudoku. However, many solvers begin by using a scanning strategy called cross-hatching.

The Cross-Hatching Strategy   Cross-hatching **involves** looking at the givens in the puzzle. Remember, there is only one of each digit in each row and column. If there is already a 2 in a column, a 2 cannot appear anywhere else in the same column. You can use this logic to find some of the missing numbers.

Look at Practice Puzzle 2. Try out the cross-hatching strategy with this puzzle.

Practice Puzzle 2

	4					6	3	
		7	8			6		5
2	6			4			8	
8			6		1		5	
		5				1		
	3		2		4			8
	5			1			3	6
6		1			7	2		
		4	9				1	

To use cross-hatching, look for numbers that appear frequently in the puzzle. You might notice that the givens in this puzzle include several 6s.

Next, look for a block that does not contain that number. For example, Block H does not include a 6. Based on the Sudoku rule, you know that a 6 must appear once in the block.

There are 6s in Columns 4 and 6 and Rows 7 and 8.

Use cross-hatching to draw imaginary lines from these 6s. These lines show where 6s cannot be. The lines are shown in this diagram.

The lines help you **conclude** that there is only one possible square in Block H where a 6 can go. The square is shaded.

Figure out where the 6 has to go in Block D. You can use cross-hatching on a separate piece of paper to find the answer.

The Doubles Strategy Finding doubles is another scanning strategy that many solvers use to **achieve** success. Doubles are the same digit that appears in two out of three blocks in a vertical or horizontal line. For example, Blocks A, B, and C form a horizontal line. Blocks B, E, and H form a vertical line.

Here is one example of the doubles strategy. It shows how logical thinking can help you **isolate** the only possible position for a number:

Many daily newspapers provide Sudoku puzzles.

- Look at Practice Puzzle 3.
- Blocks A, D, and G form a vertical line.
- There are 5s in Blocks A and G.
- There must also be a 5 in Block D. It must be in a column not used by the 5s in Blocks A and G.
- The 5 in Block D must be in Column 2.
- It could be in Row 5 or Row 6.
- However, the 5 in Block E rules out Row 5.
- Therefore, there is only one possible square for the 5 in Block D. It must be in Row 6.

Practice Puzzle 3

6		5				3	1	
	3							5
2	1			5				
	8		7		9			6
		7	4		5	1		
9			1		6		7	
				1			8	3
5							9	
	4	3				7		2

Logical thinking can help you place the 5 in Block D.

Try scanning for doubles to start solving this puzzle. Notice the 1s in Blocks C and F. See how they help you find the right place for the 1 in Block I.

Some people like to scan in numerical order. Begin with the 1s, then move to the 2s, 3s, and so on. Other people follow a more open approach. They follow their instincts and hunches.

VOCABULARY

achieve (uh CHEEV) *v.* to be successful in a particular kind of job or activity

isolate (EYE suh layt) *v.* to separate an idea, word, or problem so that it can be examined or dealt with by itself

Another part of scanning is counting. You can count the digits in a row, column, or block. Counting helps you **obtain** an answer based on which digits are missing.

Begin by counting in rows, columns, or blocks that have only a few empty squares. Look for sections of the Sudoku that are almost completed. When there are fewer possibilities, it can be easier to find the hidden numbers.

Look at Column 8 in Practice Puzzle 4. There are empty squares in Rows 2, 5, and 7. You can count to find out that the digits 3, 6, and 7 are missing in this column.

Practice Puzzle 4

	2	7			9	8	4	
9	1	6			4			
			6				1	
2	8		3				9	
3			8	9	1			2
	7				5		8	3
	9				6			
			4			6	2	9
	6	3	9			4	5	

Use cross-hatching to see that there are already 6s in Rows 2 and 7. Therefore, the 6 in Column 8 must go in Row 5.

As you solve a Sudoku, remember to **adjust** your scanning to include the numbers you have added.

These tourists try to solve a large Sudoku puzzle in Times Square in New York City.

Build on the numbers you add. The numbers you find help you narrow the possibilities in the rest of the puzzle.

Pursue your goal with patience. If you get stuck, try moving to another area of the puzzle. Switch from scanning rows to counting in blocks. If you get really stuck, take a break. Come back in ten minutes, an hour, or tomorrow. A fresh mind will help you find fresh answers.

VOCABULARY

obtain (uhb TAYN) *v.* to get something that you want, especially through your own effort, skill, or work

adjust (uh JUST) *v.* to gradually get used to a new situation by making small changes to the way you do things

pursue (puhr SOO) *v.* to continue doing an activity or trying to achieve something over a long period of time

When the Scanning Stops

Some Sudoku can be solved by scanning only. They are considered easy level puzzles. More challenging puzzles require additional types of logical thinking. You need to think through the possibilities. You might be able to **minimize** the number of squares where a number can appear, but you may not know its exact location. Many solvers jot down tiny numbers to show these possibilities.

Look at Practice Puzzle 5. You know that Block D is missing a 1. Cross-hatching helps you rule out Column 3 and Row 5. However, there are still two squares in Row 6 where the 1 might go. The puzzle shows how you can write a tiny 1 in each square. Only one of the positions is correct. Writing down the possibilities can help you remember your reasoning.

Another strategy is to write the numbers that are not possible. Solvers who do difficult puzzles often prefer

Practice Puzzle 5

6				2			5	
		9	4					2
	7	1	3			4		
7	6				8			
	3	5					2	1
1	1		2				6	7
		7			6	3	4	
9					4	7		
	4			7				9

this method. A square begins empty. Then, you start to add tiny numbers that cannot be correct. Eventually, there is just one number left to write.

Not all solvers like to write tiny numbers in their grids. Some people find that the numbers **distract** them from the correct numbers. Try using them when you solve this puzzle. Then, you can decide if you find them more helpful or annoying.

Remember, Sudoku is not a guessing game. However, a special kind of guessing can help you solve tough problems. Follow a "What-If" trail. Ask yourself: "What if I write a 7 in this square?" Follow the logical trail. If you find a conflict, you know that your original guess cannot be correct. This can be helpful when you have narrowed the choices to two or three numbers.

VOCABULARY

minimize (MIN i myz) v. to make the degree or amount of something as small as possible

distract (di STRAKT) v. draw attention away in another direction

Sudoku and Beyond

Once you have solved a few Sudoku puzzles, you can try one of these strategies to add variety:

- Solve with a partner. **Maximize** your brain power by working with a friend. Take turns adding numbers to a Sudoku puzzle.

- Beat the clock. Keep track of how long it takes you to solve a puzzle. Try to beat your own best time record.

- Challenge a friend. Make a copy of a puzzle for another puzzle solver. Begin at the same time and see who can finish first.

- Create your own. Try to fill a 9x9 grid with numbers that follow the Sudoku rule.

Some puzzle makers **adapt** the game to create new variations. For example, Practice Puzzle 6 looks very different from a traditional Sudoku because it has shapes instead of numbers. However, this change does not **affect** the logic at all. You can follow the same strategies you learned for numbers once you know all the possible shapes.

Practice Puzzle 6

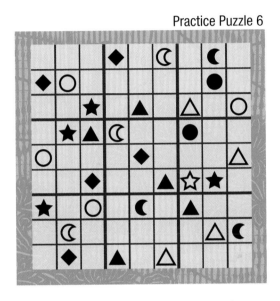

If you like doing Sudoku, you do not have to worry about running out of puzzles. Experts calculate that there are 6,670,903,752,021,072,936,960 (more than six sextillion) different ways to fill the 9x9 grid!

VOCABULARY

maximize (MAK suh myz) *v.* to increase something as much as possible

adapt (uh DAPT) *v.* change

affect (uh FEKT) *v.* to do something that produces an effect or change in someone or something

Answers

2	6	1	9	4	3	5	7	8
9	8	4	2	5	7	3	6	1
7	3	5	6	1	8	2	4	9
6	2	9	3	8	4	7	1	5
3	5	8	7	6	1	4	9	2
4	1	7	5	2	9	8	3	6
5	7	3	1	9	2	6	8	4
1	4	2	8	3	6	9	5	7
8	9	6	4	7	5	1	2	3

5	4	8	7	9	6	3	2	1
9	1	7	8	2	3	6	4	5
2	6	3	1	4	5	7	8	9
8	9	2	6	7	1	4	5	3
4	7	5	3	8	9	1	6	2
1	3	6	2	5	4	9	7	8
7	5	9	4	1	2	8	3	6
6	8	1	5	3	7	2	9	4
3	2	4	9	6	8	5	1	7

6	7	5	2	9	4	3	1	8
8	3	9	6	7	1	2	4	5
2	1	4	8	5	3	9	6	7
4	8	1	7	2	9	5	3	6
3	6	7	4	8	5	1	2	9
9	5	2	1	3	6	8	7	4
7	9	6	5	1	2	4	8	3
5	2	8	3	4	7	6	9	1
1	4	3	9	6	8	7	5	2

5	2	7	1	3	9	8	4	6
9	1	6	7	8	4	2	3	5
8	3	4	6	5	2	9	1	7
2	8	1	3	6	7	5	9	4
3	4	5	8	9	1	7	6	2
6	7	9	2	4	5	1	8	3
4	9	2	5	1	6	3	7	8
1	5	8	4	7	3	6	2	9
7	6	3	9	2	8	4	5	1

6	8	4	7	2	9	1	5	3
3	5	9	4	6	1	8	7	2
2	7	1	3	8	5	4	9	6
7	6	2	5	1	8	9	3	4
4	3	5	6	9	7	2	1	8
1	9	8	2	4	3	5	6	7
8	2	7	9	5	6	3	4	1
9	1	6	8	3	4	7	2	5
5	4	3	1	7	2	6	8	9

Discussion Questions

1. Do you think that the skills you learn to solve Sudoku can help you solve conflicts in real life? Consider when you might use such skills and strategies as scanning to gather information, narrowing the possibilities for a solution, and pursuing a goal with patience.

2. The author states that some people "follow their instincts and hunches" to solve Sudoku. Discuss the role of logical thinking versus instincts and hunches in dealing with conflicts.

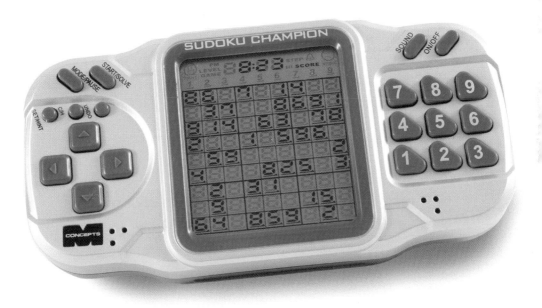

Glossary

accomplish (uh KAHM plish) *v.* to succeed in doing something, especially after trying very hard **63**

achieve (uh CHEEV) *v.* to be successful in a particular kind of job or activity **10, 66**

adapt (uh DAPT) *v.* change **73**

adjust (uh JUST) *v.* to gradually get used to a new situation by making small changes to the way you do things **8, 68**

affect (uh FEKT) *v.* to do something that produces an effect or change in someone or something **73**

anticipate (an TIS uh payt) *v.* to expect an event or situation to happen, and do something to prepare for it **55**

apparent (uh PER uhnt) *adj.* easily noticed or understood **27**

appreciate (uh PREE shee ayt) *v.* to understand or enjoy the good qualities or value of someone or something **43**

attain (uh TAYN) *v.* to succeed in reaching a particular level or in getting something after trying for a long time **42**

awe (AW) *n.* mixed feelings of fear and wonder **27**

coaxed (KOHKST) *v.* used gentle persuasion **45**

conclude (kuhn KLOOD) *v.* to form an opinion or make a judgment based on evidence presented **65**

consolation (kahn suh LAY shuhn) *n.* something that comforts a disappointed person **41**

credible (KRED uh buhl) *adj.* easy to believe **20**

demonstrate (DEM uhn strayt) *v.* to show or prove something clearly **48**

deprived (dee PRYVD) *adj.* not having the things that are necessary **36**

destiny (DES tuh nee) *n.* fate; preplanned course of events **23**

devastating (DEV uh stayt ing) *adj.* destructive; overwhelming **45**

dispelled (di SPELD) *adj.* driven away; made to disappear **14**

display (di SPLAY) *v.* to clearly show a feeling, attitude, or quality by what you do or say **33, 46**

distract (di STRAKT) *v.* draw attention away in another direction **71**

emerged (ee MERJD) *v.* came out from somewhere **36**

emphasize (EM fuh syz) *v.* to show that an opinion, idea, or quality is especially important **37, 52**

establish (uh STAB lish) *v.* to make sure of; to determine **61**

exertion (eg ZER shuhn) *n.* physical work **18**

exhibit (eg ZIB it) *v.* to show a particular quality, sign, or emotion so that it is easy to notice **55**

huddled (HUD uhld) *adj.* crowded or nestled close together **17, 30**

illustrates (IL uh strayts) *v.* to make the meaning of something clearer by giving examples **62**

ignore (ig NOHR) *v.* pay no attention to **48**

immensely (i MENS lee) *adv.* a great deal; very much **17**

impress (im PRES) *v.* to affect someone, especially by making them feel admiration and respect for you **60**

impromptu (im PRAHMP too) *adj.* unscheduled; unplanned **45**

indicate (IN di kayt) *v.* to point something out or point to
something **12, 18**

instinct (IN stinkt) *n.* a natural ability or tendency to behave
or react in a particular way, without having to learn it or
thing about it **16**

interplanetary (in tuhr PLAN uh ter ee) *adj.* between
planets **23**

intricate (IN tri kit) *adj.* complex; detailed **63**

involves (in VAHLVZ) *v.* includes something as a necessary
part or result **64**

isolate (EYE suh layt) *v.* to make a place separate from other
places so that people cannot enter it **17, 66**

laborious (luh BOHR ee uhs) *adj.* taking much work
or effort **8**

malicious (muh LISH uhs) *adj.* spiteful; hateful **42**

maximize (MAK suh myz) *v.* to increase something as much
as possible **72**

minimize (MIN i myz) *v.* to make the degree or amount of
something as small as possible **70**

neglected (ni GLEKT uhd) *adj.* not taken care of **34**

objects (AHB jekts) *n.* things that can be seen or
touched **19**

observe (uhb ZERV) *v.* to watch someone or something
carefully **27**

obtain (uhb TAYN) *v.* to get something that you want,
especially through your own effort, skill, or work **68**

perpetual (puhr PECH oo uhl) *adj.* constant; unending **48** plausible (PLAW zuh buhl) *adj.* seemingly true; acceptable **21**

plot (PLAHT) *n.* the sequence of events in a story **53**

predict (pree DIKT) *v.* to say what is going to happen in the future, based on available information or past experience **28**

promote (pruh MOHT) *v.* to help something develop and be successful **60**

pursue (puhr SOO) *v.* to continue doing an activity or trying to achieve something over a long period of time **29, 69**

react (ree AKT) *v.* to behave in a particular way because of something that has happened or something that has been said to you **29**

rely (ree LY) *v.* to trust someone or something to do what you need or expect them to do **53**

remote (ree MOHT) *adj.* far away from everything else **14, 36**

research (REE serch) *n.* serious study of a subject, that is intended to discover new facts or test new ideas **21**

research (REE serch) *v.* to study a subject in detail, especially in order to discover new facts or test new ideas **24**

reveal (ree VEEL) *v.* to show something that was previously hidden **8**

simultaneously (sy muhl TAY nee uhs lee) *adv.* at the same time **60**

solemn (SAHL uhm) *adj.* serious; somber **28, 41**

spectators (SPEK tayt uhrz) *n.* onlookers **27**

subject (SUB jikt) *n.* the main idea or topic **52**

survive (ser VYV) *v.* to continue to exist in spite of many difficulties and dangers **18, 29**

timid (TIM id) *adj.* showing shyness **51**

verify (VER uh fy) *v.* to check whether or not something is true **7, 34, 63**

Photo Credits

Cover: t.l. George H. H. Huey/CORBIS; **t.m.** NASA Johnson Space Center (NASA-JSC); **t.r.** Getty Images; **b.** Getty Images; **4: t.** George H. H. Huey/CORBIS; **4–5: b.** George H. H. Huey/ CORBIS; **6:** Tom Bean/CORBIS; **7:** W. Wayne Lockwood, M.D./ CORBIS; **8–9:** Richard Cummins/CORBIS; **10–11:** George H. H. Huey/CORBIS; **12–13:** Liz Hymans/CORBIS; **14–15:** Atlantide Phototravel/CORBIS; **16:** George H. H. Huey/CORBIS; **19: l.** George H. H. Huey/CORBIS ; **19: r.** George H. H. Huey/ CORBIS; **19. m.** George H. H. Huey/CORBIS; **20:** Beth Wald/ Aurora & Quanta Productions, Inc.; **22:** Tiziou Jacques/CORBIS Sygma; **23:** NASA Johnson Space Center (NASA-JSC); **25:** NASA Johnson Space Center (NASA-JSC); **26:** © Bettmann/CORBIS; **28:** © CORBIS; **31:** © Bureau L.A. Collection/CORBIS; **32:** Digital image © 1996 CORBIS; Original image courtesy of NASA/CORBIS; **33: l.** Bill Eppridge/Time & Life Pictures/Getty Images; **33: r.** AP/ Wide World Photos; **35:** © Dorling Kindersley; **36: b.** © Bettmann/ CORBIS; **36:** inset NASA Johnson Space Center (NASA-JSC); **37:** © Bettmann/CORBIS; **38:** NASA Johnson Space Center (NASA-JSC); **40:** Royalty-free/CORBIS; **42:** Richard Cummins/CORBIS; **44:** CORBIS; **47:** Bettmann/CORBIS; **49: m.** Kevin Fleming/ CORBIS; **49: l.** Courtesy of the Library of Congress; **49: r.** Bettmann/ CORBIS; **50–51:** Hulton-Deutsch Collection/CORBIS; **52:** Courtesy of the Library of Congress; **54:** Felix Heyder/dpa/CORBIS; **56:** Buddy Mays/CORBIS; **57:** Don Mason/CORBIS; **58–59:** Getty Images; **60:** PhotoDisc, Inc./Getty Images; **61:** AFP/Getty Images; **66:** AP/ Wide World; **69:** Getty Images; **71:** Getty Images; **72:** Getty Images